AVALON VISIONS

AVALON VISIONS ORACLE
Sacred Wisdom Through the Three Realms

Copyright © 2026 Cheryl Yambrach Rose

All rights reserved. Except for personal use, no part of this publication may be reproduced, in whole or in part, without written permission from the publisher. These cards are for spiritual and emotional guidance only and are not a substitute for medical advice or treatment. The author's views, within and beyond this publication, do not necessarily reflect those of the publisher. We respectfully request that this content not be used to train AI-generative models or machine learning systems without the publisher's written consent.

Published by Blue Angel Publishing®
10 Trafford Court, Wheelers Hill,
Victoria, Australia 3150
E-mail: info@blueangelonline.com
Website: www.blueangelonline.com

Edited by Cherise Asmah and Jules Sutherland

Blue Angel is a registered trademark of Blue Angel Gallery Pty Ltd.

ISBN: 978-1-922574-55-8

Printed on sustainably sourced paper,
with soy-based inks.

CHERYL YAMBRACH ROSE

AVALON VISIONS ORACLE

Sacred Wisdom Through the Three Realms

CONTENTS

...

FOREWORD 9

THE REALMS OF AVALON 11
Card Spreads 15

CARD MEANINGS:
OTHERWORLD CARDS 23

1. Parting the Mists of Avalon 24
2. Arthur Under the Tor 26
3. The Swan Maiden 28
4. The Secret Well 30
5. The Portal Beckons 32

6. Avalon Garden Deva 34
7. Wick Hollow 36
8. Manannán mac Lir 38
9. King Uther and the Dragon's Breath 40
10. Avalon Oracle 42
11. The Tor Gate 44

CARD MEANINGS: TERRESTRIAL WORLD CARDS 47

12. Magdalene Close 48
13. Winter Solstice 50
14. Arthur's Footprint 52
15. Priestess Blessing 54
16. Guinevere 56
17. Arthur at Tintagel 58
18. Cernunnos 60
19. Magog 62
20. Dinas Emrys 64
21. Cerridwen's Cauldron 66
22. Imbolc 68
23. The Initiation of Arthur 70
24. Beltane 72
25. The Nine Morgans 74
26. Lughnasa 76
27. Brigantia 78
28. The Three Grails 80
29. Avnova 82

30. Epona **84**
31. The Egg Stone **86**
32. Beckery and the Blue Spring **88**
33. Song of Branwen **90**
34. Celtic Shamanka **92**
35. Green Men of Glastonbury **94**

CARD MEANINGS: STELLAR WORLD CARDS **97**

36. Elen of the Ways **98**
37. The Arrival of the Tuatha Dé Danann **100**
38. Caer Arianrhod **104**
39. Morgan, High Priestess of Avalon **106**
40. Archangel Michael **108**
41. Taygetan Warrior **110**
42. Angel of Chalice Well **112**
43. Silbury Stargate **114**
44. Chalice Well Continuum **116**

ABOUT THE AUTHOR/ARTIST **119**

FOREWORD
BY
GEOFFREY ASHE MBE FRSL

• • •

I FIRST BECAME AWARE OF CHERYL WHEN LOOKING at a collection of work by several artists associated with Mt. Shasta. Her work stood out from the rest and aroused my curiosity. Afterwards, I happened to meet Cheryl when she visited Glastonbury, and I used pictures of hers to illustrate a book of my own (*Atlantis*, Thames and Hudson). I have since helped in guiding several of her tours.

Much of Cheryl's work has been related—with notable vividness and originality—to the lore and legend of Arthurian Britain. While many artists have interpreted Arthurian themes, they have seldom come as close as they might to the reality of actual places, or evoked the kind of imagery that can arise if they are allowed to make their impact freely. Cheryl has been highly successful in this way, beautifully exploring the realms of myth and symbol without ever sacrificing firmness of outline, graphic power, and closeness of visible fact.

THE REALMS OF AVALON

• • •

AVALON IS A PLACE WHERE THE MISTS PART AND THE veils become transparent. All exists here in 'the time of no time'. Those with psychic abilities or 'the Sight' (as it's often referred to in Celtic cultures) can view these realms of the past, present, and future. The original Celtic idea of the three worlds includes sea, land, and sky, and this concept of three realms is known across the globe by different names expressing the Lower World, Middle World, and Upper World. I choose to present them in the Neo-Mythic concept of the Otherworld, Terrestrial World, and Stellar World. This reflects the notion that none are lower or higher but rather, they are integrated into the matrix or Sourcefield of today, where they exist simultaneously and can be accessed by all.

This oracle encompasses those three realms of Celtic spirituality centered around Glastonbury:

THE OTHERWORLD is where different creative expressions bubble up from the waters of Gaia's inner earth through magical wells and springs. It is a place of inspiration where gifts and knowledge are brought back to the surface through 'the hero's journey' of transformation.

THE TERRESTRIAL WORLD is the land of nature, where many diverse animals, plants, humans, and other living beings interconnect and occupy the surface world of this planet.

THE STELLAR WORLD is where interstellar communications come down from above through celestial beings, astrology, and the different races of our star family. This world has been co-opted by religions and shrouded in dogma for centuries. Now, it is time to look up and expand your own universe with enhanced perception.

Within every person is a multisensory being. These cards will liberate your inner knowing and build pathways through word and image to connect you to the infinite wisdom of Source. There are no timelines or levels to go up and down — that is linear thinking and a human concept. The three worlds of the Celts exist all at once and are intricately interwoven.

This deck was painted in Glastonbury and in my castle studio in Northern Ireland overlooking the Irish Sea. I created this oracle deck by reaching into the continuum of the sacred sites of Avalon and seeing what is held within its grid. I paint the multi/higher-dimensional experience of the sites along with the historical data. I have joyfully drawn on many decades of experiences and visions in Southwest Britain and Wales to bring into being a powerful portal for readings.

NEO-MYTHIC ART

• • •

I founded the art style 'Neo-Mythic Art' to express 'The New Myth' — the bringing of ancient myth into the present field of time and space. Sometimes the painting is looking at the present from a future perspective, as history, and sometimes it is looking at past history in contemporary terms. Some paintings are a little of both.

As a tour guide in the UK for 20 years, I realized I had always been working this way. An example of this happened on Midsummer at Cadbury/Camelot in Somerset. Arthur and his companions rode through, as they were known to do at that time of year. The horses' hooves were SO loud hitting the old stone road that was once there, that we all jumped out of the way! The thing is, the road is now dirt, but the sound echoed like it was bouncing off the walls of a tunnel. I was holding one of the old, worn paving stones, calling to Arthur when it happened. This is an example of previous times bleeding through to this time-frame reference, and provides ongoing inspiration to paint what I continue to experience in my Arthurian and Avalon paintings.

After each card message, you will find a passage called 'Neo-Mythic Bridge'. This is the background story on each painting, and how it represents the past/present/future Avalon continuum.

CARD SPREADS

• • •

Where you can, I recommend taking the cards to what I call 'power points' on the earth. Let them absorb the energy of Gaia's breath upon them. I always feel readings are more profound in sacred surroundings — out on the land, where the energy lines or the veins and arteries of our planet can be accessed.

THE THREE REALMS

This simple, three-card spread offers you messages from each of the three realms—the Otherworld, the Terrestrial World, and the Stellar World—giving you multidimensional guidance from the Avalon continuum.

First, separate the cards into the three groups using the Realms symbols on the cards:

Then shuffle each pile while thinking of your question.

CARD ONE: Pick one card from the Otherworld group and lay this down on the left. You can also think of this as a message from the sea, something in the unconscious that is trying to rise to the surface of your awareness.

CARD TWO: Then, choose a card from the Terrestrial World pile and place it in the centre. This card represents a message from the land—the animals, plants, and guides of the surface world—and ways to bring this wisdom into your everyday life.

CARD THREE: Lastly, pick a card from the Stellar World group and place it on the right. This card holds a message from the sky or celestial realms — interstellar communication speaking directly to your higher self with supportive guidance.

The Tor

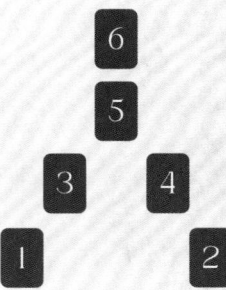

This spread assists in stepping over the threshold and unlocking the gateway to change. This can apply to a location, business, relationships, partnerships, and life changes in general.

Card One: Climbing the steps of the Tor, my focus is … ?
Card Two: How is this change serving my highest good?
Card Three: What are the obstacles to this change?
Card Four: What or who influences this change?
Card Five: How can I go through this shift with grace and ease?
Card Six: As I stand in the tower, what will the wind carry up and away that I no longer need?

MORGAN'S PORTAL

Think of a question you would like to ask the High Priestess of Avalon. This is a good spread for lovers and family issues.

CARD ONE: Influences from other people.
CARD TWO: Personal issues.
CARD THREE: Insights.
CARD FOUR: What I want.
CARD FIVE: Outcome.
CARD SIX: Message from the High Priestess.

THE SACRED WELL

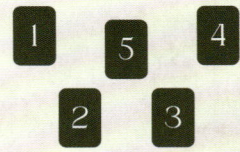

This layout can be applied to finding your soul path. Look through the cards and choose one that best represents this question for you and place it in the center. Let the answers bubble up from the great reservoir of Gaia's wisdom.

CARD ONE: What blocks my progress?
CARD TWO: What issues need to be resolved to move forward?
CARD THREE: What actions will assist me?
CARD FOUR: What do I fear?
CARD FIVE: What represents my soul path?

THROUGH THE VEILS OF THE YEAR

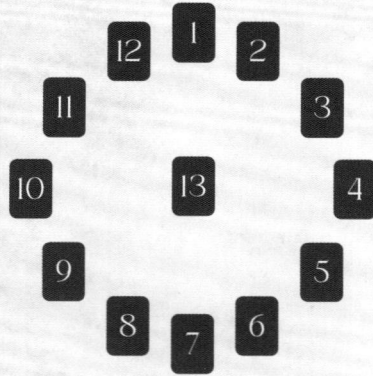

A twelve-month spread of insights that may influence your year. Lay out 12 cards in a circle with 13th card in the middle representing the overall guidance. You may want to take a photo of the reading to refer back to as the year progresses, reflecting on the message for each month.

Card Meanings

Otherworld Cards

1. PARTING THE MISTS OF AVALON

...

Answer the Calling

FEEL CONFIDENT — THE MISTS ARE PARTING! The things that have been previously shrouded in mystery and beyond your reach are now becoming visible to you. You have worked hard and learned your lessons well. New encounters and insights await just beyond the mist. It is time to move forward into the realm of infinite possibilities. Take that first step and do not falter or be influenced by others who are mired in their own fog. While they may value widely accepted paradigms and belief systems, these do not resonate with your own wisdom and inner knowing. There is no right or wrong in this, just different journeys and perspectives; each individual identifying with their own choices and path. You know yours well, and you have waited years for this moment. So go now; sail on and embrace it. Welcome home!

Neo-Mythic Bridge

The Isle of Avalon was originally called Ynis Witrin. It is an old British term for the Isle of Glass — this is where Glastonbury got its name. A 500-foot hill called the Tor rises up out of the watery marshes and seems to float in the shifting tides and clouds. The hill has been formed into a seven-terrace Cretan spiral labyrinth thought to be a ritual path dating from the 2nd or 3rd millennium BCE. This creates a contact point with the Celtic Otherworld. The Druid symbol of Awen is carved into a stone representing the three sunrise positions of the equinoxes.

2. ARTHUR UNDER THE TOR

...

A Deep Connection Emerges

SOMEONE FROM YOUR PAST IS TRYING TO communicate. There is a past-life issue ready to be realized and integrated. This will help you understand and resolve some current matters you question in your life. You now have access to the wellspring of Avalon and beyond to discern why you have journeyed to this point, either physically or psychically. Arthur—who is ever-living—speaks to you from his subterranean kingdom under the Tor. Look deeply into his eyes and bring back what is stirring in the cellular memory of your heart. There is something lost that can be found again to serve you in this lifetime.

A vision received remotely can be just as powerful since extrasensory telepathy knows no time or distance. Remember this and tune in. Your higher self or superconscious mind speaks in its own language of symbols and archetypes. These contain a code you will have to decipher to unlock, and only you can do it. You may use your favorite divinatory tools just to open the door and reveal the path. King Arthur has appeared in your reading to help you cross the threshold.

Neo-Mythic Bridge

Annwn is a place of everlasting life and abundance. In a sense, it is a paradise located deep within the earth. This realm is also referred to as the Celtic Otherworld, and is ruled by Gwyn ap Nudd. Arthur traversed this landscape in many tales. He was able to enter and return to the surface world. It is said there is an entrance near Glastonbury Tor.

3. THE SWAN MAIDEN

• • •

Transformation

EVERYONE HAS THE DIVINE RIGHT TO FREEDOM. Beware those who would try to limit you with their own expectations and desires. Start afresh. You didn't choose to incarnate here to repeat the decisions and patterns of your past existences. Free your soul and fly, for you, like the swan maiden, are a bridge between worlds. You too can shapeshift from the mundane Terrestrial World to the Otherworld and back again. Vibrate to a higher frequency where you can envision your wings. No one can catch you if they don't resonate and match your frequency! Say no to any agendas that feel off — if it doesn't feel right to you, it isn't. You know your own mind and are capable of reinventing yourself and your life. Transmute, transform, spread your wings and fly!

Neo-Mythic Bridge
On the Somerset levels of Avalon, the light and the mist create an ethereal landscape with shifting patterns on the water. Here in the reeds, the swan maiden hides from predators. Her purity and grace are sought by those who wish to possess her. When she removes her feather cloak to swim in the water as a human woman, the covetous hunters sneak up and grab her cloak and hide it so she cannot return. Once the swan maiden finds her feathery garment, she is released from the bonds that held her and once again free to fly with her chosen soul family.

4. THE SECRET WELL

...

Disruption

Your inner turmoil is stirring you to take action now and forge your personal destiny. A necessary change needs to be made. Take the reins before it is likely forced upon you — the outcome will be worse if you let fear hold you back from proactively reshaping old habits and situations.

It is said Gwyn ap Nudd masters the weather and the winds of change. To resist him for the sake of convenience and security invites his lightning rod of disruption into your world. It is better to permit the change to take place and adjust your life accordingly. You can navigate gently through the obstacles one by one, always considering the best way of moving forward that will have the least impact on yourself and others.

Keep calm. Remember, disruption does not necessarily mean destruction, but can be a way of presenting new possibilities you might not have noticed previously.

Neo-Mythic Bridge

Gwyn ap Nudd returns through a secret portal to his realm under the Glastonbury Tor, deep into the hillside. Gwyn must spend time there in the darkness of winter. This duration in the Otherworld cannot be avoided and is part of the rhythm and flow of the Terrestrial World. The Lynx is known as a keeper of secrets and is believed to have multidimensional eyesight that allows the cat to see through the three worlds, making it a perfect guardian for this entrance. This secret well is a recent rediscovery in Glastonbury town and has been hidden for a long time, as it is difficult to get to and not easily seen.

5. THE PORTAL BECKONS

...

Retreat

Find peace by tuning in to a higher-frequency version of yourself. Some people might covet the light you carry, but you are stronger than you know. Leave behind those who cannot (or will not) change for the better. If you find yourself embroiled in a relationship that takes more than it gives (whether it is with a romantic partner, friend, or co-worker), begin to withdraw your energy as soon as you can when it does not feel right. Sometimes the signs may look like a spiral, as repeated behaviours that eventually become less subtle. Gather your internal resources. Use your heart-brain to discern what is conducive to your soul's purpose and stick with that. Seek respite in the wisdom of your higher self and those in your community who will stand by your sovereignty and growth. You are a powerful being and your own master.

Neo-Mythic Bridge

When the terrestrial human population became intolerable, the Tuatha Dé Danann (a supernatural race) found sanctuary in the Otherworld. After many battles, the Tuatha Dé Danann decided to retreat to a realm of peace for their people. They sometimes return to the surface world and are occasionally seen near ancient mounds.

6. AVALON GARDEN DEVA

...

Observe and Listen

THERE IS MOVEMENT ALL AROUND YOU. STOP FOR a moment and listen. Feel the deep currents and influences that are affecting your life and personal environment. Ask the subtle energies in nature to communicate what needs to be done. You will know the answer intuitively when it comes through.

The Deva looks hesitant to engage here — even surprised you can see her. The elementals do not automatically love humans, for they are wary of their destructive nature. Comfort her with your actions by nurturing your garden or environment in some way. She will respond in kind.

The delicacy of flowers is worth your contemplation and protection. They are a physical example of a magical merging of the three worlds with their roots below and the flower above, reaching for the heavens. Adapt to the devic world instead of expecting them to adapt only to yours. This shift in thinking will truly expand your perception and inner sight.

Neo-Mythic Bridge

We know plants are sentient beings that can react to our love or anger. Perhaps this is because each one of them has a guardian elemental spirit. In the crown adorning our Deva is one of the first plants to appear in the Glastonbury garden in spring. It is called the Lords-and-Ladies. This amazing plant is both male and female and has become a symbol of Beltane. The Divine Feminine flower cradles the Divine Masculine in her green chalice.

7. WICK HOLLOW

...

An Invitation Beckons

A journey awaits you. This may change your perception of life as you know it. Forget your known programs and accepted paradigms for a moment to explore. Close your eyes and enter the green tunnel. Your imagination runs wild as ancient memories stir. Feel the portals around you open up into the supernatural realm of the Otherworld. The animals watch you from their secret hiding places, knowing the Mother Goddess is there to protect them.

You may choose to accept or reject the invitation to traverse between the worlds. If you accept, a sacred gift will be given to you as you finish your journey within the magical realms. It is for you to bring back to the Terrestrial World. Some will not listen to you or believe your experiences. But you carry this treasure of Avalon inside you, and you understand that sharing it will stimulate the consciousness and enhance the everyday life of the people that you come in contact with. This could be achieved through art, music, writing, or other modalities that you wish to use.

Neo-Mythic Bridge

The processional path to the Tor through Wick Hollow has a primordial feeling, with creatures calling out on the right and left. Foxes and owls can be heard with badgers scurrying into the bushes as you pass. Trees grow sideways out of the cliff face like walls, creating an eerie atmosphere. Couples often tryst there, hidden beneath the leafy bowers.

8. MANANNÁN MAC LIR

...

New Discoveries

YOU HAVE THE KEYS TO UNLOCK THE DOORS TO AN expanded awareness. Be open to new discoveries by considering the existence of other realities. There is so much still unknown to us — veiled, cloaked, and hidden from sight. When you are near the vastness of the ocean, remember it is part of the Otherworld and ponder how much is waiting to be experienced.

Ancient texts and carvings record the presence of otherworldly beings in times when 'gods and men' walked side by side and fairy folk lived among the mortals. These are your fairy allies, who occupy the same space as you and are there for you to call forth. They love it when you honor them with rituals, such as creating an altar of natural and precious ornaments in your garden or the forest. Try dressing in fey costume and attending a fairy ball or event. Masks and fantasy costumes allow you the freedom to try out a different scenario in another reality and have fun!

As you evolve and raise your frequency, you can look forward to living consciously among other races and deities once more. Perhaps you can see them already! Bring your new skills from this contact into your life and creations. This will allow them to once again live in the Terrestrial World and in the consciousness of others.

Neo-Mythic Bridge

Some of the fey races are sea people. They were once assumed to be gods, as everyone who didn't look like a human was called a god. Sea gods or 'fish men' hailing from kingdoms under the ocean are recorded in almost every culture throughout history, such as the Sumerian Enki, Poseidon, the Dogon ancestral spirits called Nommo, and of course, mermaids and mermen.

9. KING UTHER AND THE DRAGON'S BREATH

...

Destiny

Take up your sword of power and use it wisely. If you believe it is predestination, then go for it — being fully aware that there is no going back. Do keep in mind how your actions will affect the others around you as you proceed. Be on the lookout for signs and symbols that represent your fate. Symbols speak in a language of their own to stimulate your intuitive self. When the conscious mind is engaged and focused on an image, the door is open to go deeper and receive ideas and thoughts from your higher self. You can then translate the symbols into meanings that pertain to your situation and fate.

Be mindful of astral entities who might enter through your open portal, wanting to influence you and your life to work out their own agendas. Your destiny belongs to you alone. Call on King Uther's sword of protection to keep your psychic firewall all around you as you move forward with your plans.

Neo-Mythic Bridge

Uther became High King of the Britons. Uther's name, Pendragon, literally means "head dragon" in the original Brittonic language. (This later became a title for head leader, which was inherited by his son, Arthur.) It is said he took this name after he witnessed a prophetic dragon-shaped comet shoot across the night sky. He believed this event foretold his destiny as high commander of Britain.

10. AVALON ORACLE

...

You Are Not Alone

You have been brave, sometimes courageous, in very difficult circumstances, but now it is time to ask for help. You cannot do it all by yourself. Turning to a wise elder, a beloved deity, or friend for advice is not defeat; it is a way of thinking outside yourself and objectively considering other ideas and solutions. The Priestess of Avalon asks the Oracle, when she is really asking her higher self through that medium. Consulting a divine being that you deeply connect with, or seeking counsel from someone you hold in high esteem, can manifest pointers and guidelines to help you find your own way through the quagmire of a seemingly impossible situation. Confiding in someone you trust will lighten your burden. If the problem must stay private, you can also get help by reading a favorite author you resonate with, focusing on an inspiring artwork, quietly meditating while listening to a piece of music, or using the spreads in this oracle deck, allowing your higher self to have a voice and break through to you.

Neo-Mythic Bridge

Oracles as vehicles have occupied Avalon and her magic springs and wells from time immemorial. The veils are thin, and the energy of the landscape is conducive to visions and prophecy.

11. THE TOR GATE

...

The Portal Is Opening

IT IS TIME TO END ONE CYCLE AND BEGIN THE NEXT. Samhain is the Celtic New Year. The veils of Avalon dissolve now, allowing you to enter the Otherworld and honor the souls that have transitioned from the Terrestrial World to the Celestial Realms. However, remember that being out of the physical body—whether by death or a chosen condition—does not necessarily denote wisdom! Be discerning in who you choose to connect to, including your ancestors.

Enter through the gateway if you wish, but protect yourself at all times. Be aware of the seen and unseen energies around you. Look for the symbols and signs that represent the best way forward, and call on your known allies to support you.

Neo-Mythic Bridge

This magical gate is to the left of the original processional path up the Tor. There are apple trees and sheep grazing peacefully. The Cailleach is approaching the gate. Her hair is already turning silver. She will return to her cavern in the hillside of the Tor that is emblazoned with calcite crystals. She will rest there contemplating and meditating until spring, when she is once again reborn as the maiden, for she is the Triple Goddess.

Card Meanings

Terrestrial World Cards

12. MAGDALENE CLOSE

⋯

Nurture Others

EMPATHY AND UNDERSTANDING ARE NEEDED NOW. Sometimes it is healthy to step out of your own life to view a situation from another perspective. Have compassion and don't judge. If there is someone you are holding vigil for, picture yourself inside the chapel of Magdalene's Hospice, lighting the candles flickering in the window. Focus your thoughts and prayers on one central point or person. This concentrated energy will transcend time and distance, with information and healing thoughts traveling instantly within what is called quantum entanglement.

Compassion and love are the most powerful forces within you and in the field in which you dwell. You are a key part of it. The propensity you have within your psychic abilities could well include the gift of healing others. People open up to you because you are truthful and see things clearly. Offer this Sight to those who ask for help.

Neo-Mythic Bridge

In the center of Avalon, Glastonbury Abbey sits in ruined grandeur on Magdalene Street. Across the road is Magdalene Close and the Royal Magdalene Almshouses. These buildings are two rows of an ancient hospital and chapel. Chalice Well water once flowed through the grounds as part of the healing process. The aged oak window of the silent chapel creates a sacred atmosphere in the garden where time melts away and you can feel the presence of Mary Magdalene standing there before you.

13. WINTER SOLSTICE

⋯

Sacred Marriage

A relationship is more than the sum of its parts. Let ritual support you to deepen your love and expand the alchemy of two souls into the ecstasy of the higher realms of consciousness. Strive for both personal sovereignty and equality in your connections. Together, you can find the balance and retain your self-respect. A relationship should not define you, but enhance the life experience of both individuals.

Remember also to allow change and let the winds dance between you. It may not be an eternal alliance, but when each partner is encouraged to follow their own soul path, a harmonious synthesis is created. This is the highest love — the alchemy of true happiness that can be experienced when both partners are satisfied with their lives and sense of purpose.

Neo-Mythic Bridge

Prior to Arthur's crowning ceremony, the Great Marriage took place. Through this rite, Arthur became the *axis mundi* of his kingdom, the connection between the heavens and the earth. A priestess was selected to represent the Sovereignty Goddess in his marriage to the land. Arthur could only become a sovereign if he respected Gaia and her Divine Feminine aspect. The other priestesses held the space outside for protection through the night.

14. ARTHUR'S FOOTPRINT

...

Crown Yourself

Make sure you are prepared in body, mind, and spirit before taking on a position of power and responsibility. To assume a position of authority, you will be required to embody both the heavenly upper or Stellar World and the Otherworld—with all its aspects and challenges—in the Terrestrial World. Keep a watchful eye on ego. It is also important to integrate the masculine and feminine polarities in your decisions. Always respect and honor the guidance from your inner connection to Source.

Scrutinize your intentions carefully and stay objective through time, because the criteria for judging situations may change and you need to be able to adapt to those changes with grace and ease. In other words, stay open and remember to listen. Change is the only constant, and to be a great leader, you must learn to flow with it, even if it is not what you envisioned initially. Sticking stubbornly to old paradigms is a sure way to end up falling into the trenches of the third-dimensional world. Success is achievable with well-timed thoughts and actions.

Neo-Mythic Bridge

It is believed that the rite of sacred kingship took place on Tintagel Island in North Cornwall on Winter Solstice. The druids call this *Alban Arthuan* or the "light of Arthur". The island was considered part of the Otherworld because it was neither land nor sea but that magical place between worlds — 'betwixt and between.' The king would then place his left foot in a carved hollow footprint in the slate, connecting himself to the Great Goddess while he crowned himself in full view.

15. PRIESTESS BLESSING

...

Healing

Nurture the connection between your mind and body. Ritual can keep your consciousness at beta level, allowing you to go in, reprogram your mind and reject any previous programming that contributes to illness. Repeat the new paradigm you have created like a mantra. By using this process, you will retrain your subconscious. This can work on unhealthy habits as well. You are in control. In your mind, travel to the flowing waters to restore balance and vibrant health.

Stress and lifestyle can also shut down your immune system, keeping you in fight-or-flight mode. Stop for a moment and be still. Close your eyes and hear the robins sing as you visualize the water cascading down the rocks into the healing pool. Remember, your consciousness controls your cells. Speak to them. Your cells respond to what you tell them. They are not trapped in a genetic pattern; they can be changed and transformed into a new one. Your inner priestess will help give them hope and positive pathways to healing and well-being.

Neo-Mythic Bridge

The blood-red water of Chalice Well is primal water from deep within the earth, and carries to the surface healing properties from the Otherworld. The Priestesses stand in the sanctuary near the Pilgrim's Bath. Morgan le Fay brought Arthur to her sanctuary there and put her trained priestesses in charge of his healing, for his journey onward.

16. GUINEVERE

• • •

Confidence

You are in control of your destiny. Don't let others tell you different or make you doubt your self-worth. Guinevere's (Queen of Britain and wife of Arthur) story was rewritten by those who resented her, to diminish her value and significance. If you become truly empowered, others cannot undermine you. Take up your crown, rod of power, and sword of truth. Be the ruler of your own life. That divine sovereign is inside you, just waiting to be called forth. Call it in now! In the greatest detail possible, visualize yourself wearing a crown or taking up a sword, and feel yourself change.

Past mistakes were only life lessons to be learned, so leave them there — in the past. You have overcome them and they are experiences that have made you so strong. No one has power over you when you show them you are a sovereign being! Set a confident example for others to see.

Neo-Mythic Bridge

Guinevere was an empress in her own right, honoring the Great Goddess and representing her in the Terrestrial World. She was from Lyonesse, which was a cultural hub of exotic trade from the Mediterranean, the far east, and North Africa. She would have been exposed to many ideas from travelers, giving her an extraordinary education that would prove useful during her reign as queen.

17. ARTHUR AT TINTAGEL

...

Triumph

Conquer your adversaries with right action. Recent activities are clearing your path for you to move on to the next phase that you choose — celebrate! The self-assurance you exhibit will inspire others to keep going; they also wish to attain their goals. There is no harm in feeling proud of your achievements, as long as you continue the forward movement.

Like Arthur with his group of companions (or with his wife Guinevere), you can form a powerful alliance that benefits you and empowers all through cooperation and shared values. Your chosen actions may bring praise and accolades and be remembered in the human story as a turning point of great significance! Have courage and stand tall, embracing your ability to succeed.

Neo-Mythic Bridge

When Arthur achieves Sacred Kingship, he leaves Tintagel, proudly displaying his red dragon banner. He carries the strength of Ursa the Bear within him. Under the golden adornments, he still wears his magical sword for protection, as any wise king or queen would do. He is credited with keeping the Saxons at bay.

18. CERNUNNOS

• • •

Sexual Energy

Run wild through the forest. Celebrate the coming of new life. Dance, spin, and chant. Let loose and live. Call to the Green Man of the forest with love and passion. A fertility ritual, like many ancient ones celebrated in nature, would be powerful now. Gather herbs, moss, shells, magical plants, and personal talismans. Lay them out in a symbolic design that is meaningful to you and represents your intentions on an altar of wood or stone, or even upon the earth itself. Arrange fruits, flowers, or seeds you gather yourself from the land on which you live. Fill a chalice with wine or sacred water blessed by the Goddess of the land. Dance with words within the framework of ritual. Movement allows the mind and energy to be focused and become more powerful in its concentrated form. Call your Lord of the Dance, Cernunnos, or his representative on Earth—the Green Man or Wild Woman—into your life. Pour the contents of the chalice onto the earth or share it with your chosen partner.

Neo-Mythic Bridge

The stag usually appears in spring but this fertile energy can surface any time! Cernunnos is considered the wild god of the woodlands. He is sometimes called Herne of the wild hunt and embodies divine masculine energy. He is the protector of the forest and its inhabitants; animals and elementals alike. In Avalon, he comes out at the time of Beltane in May when Green Men appear everywhere to honor him.

19. MAGOG

...

Persevere

You must survive even though you see things falling away around you. Let your mighty grove of friends and allies combine their strength with yours to hold each other up. Like the intertwining roots of the great trees, group support is powerful during these difficult times.

The great oak Magog closes her eyes. Her oak-tree partner, Gog, died from a small candle that was lit inside him on a makeshift altar. The flame was left burning and he was consumed by fire. Magog stands alone now next to him, on the ancient druidic ceremonial path, but she still stands holding the sacred space.

Embody this unbreakable spirit of the mighty oak. Be steadfast and strong. Your roots are deep in the ground, your body traverses the landscape of Terra, and your eyes look up to the stars and planets above you. Let this integration of the three worlds balance your body and psyche to thrive under the most diverse conditions that we all face today.

Neo-Mythic Bridge

The processional way from Wick Hollow to the Tor was flanked on both sides by ancient oak trees. Some were over 2000 years old and 11 feet in diameter. The oak bridged the three worlds. The canopy reached into the upper Stellar World and its roots reached just as deep into the Otherworld beneath. The sacred ceremonies of the Druids were held within the grove. Even the word Druid literally means 'oak men.' The oldest trees left along this path are Gog and Magog.

20. DINAS EMRYS

...

You Have the Power

You don't need an intermediary — do your own readings. You are your own authority and have mastery over your fate. Own it. Reach inside and connect to the powerful being you know you truly are. Draw on your higher self and become one with Source. Use your energy wisely and with discretion. You do not need to have power over others in order to lead. Doing that without compassion and understanding is actually less skillful. Sometimes the best way of teaching is by example. Merlin and other shamans of old knew this and would create scenarios where the student could interact within the structure of story or myth. These would illuminate the teachings and allow the student to arrive at their own conclusions. This card offers such wisdom for you now, and is linked to the telluric and esoteric currents of the sacred site depicted in the artwork. Allow the power of Merlin's story to mirror the magic you contain within.

Neo-Mythic Bridge

Merlin was a real person and lived, like Arthur, in the 6th century. He is believed to be a Druid who brought technology and psychic abilities from his homeland in Atlantis. Vortigern, King of the Britons, was told by his wise men to build a castle on a crystal and copper hill. The young Emrys (Merlin) foretold that beneath the hill were two sleeping dragons and an underground lake. The red dragon represented the Britons, while the white dragon represented the Saxons. The battle was symbolic of the win over the invaders. Later, Merlin inherited the castle, which is called Dinas Emrys after him.

21. CERRIDWEN'S CAULDRON

...

Prepare for Change

Use your wisdom to get out of a difficult situation. Think quickly, but stay in control. On your way back from the Otherworld, the Dark Goddess may attempt to push you back into the abyss to sink or swim. Refuse to accept defeat — swim and experience a rebirth that will transform you in incredible ways.

When you have resurfaced, let go of all you went through. Now it is time to recover and get to work. Your priorities may have changed from your ordeals, so use that in the restructuring of your life and pursuits. You are passing out of danger even if your destination is unknown. Ask your higher self for guidance through your chosen oracle. This will raise your frequency and repel negative influences. You are free.

Neo-Mythic Bridge

Cerridwen is the Dark Goddess of wisdom and prophecy. She is the crone aspect of the Triple Goddess. It is said she lives in a glass castle under Glastonbury Tor. Her legend is about transmutation and transformation.

22. IMBOLC

...

Spring into Action

Unleash your creative powers. Plant seeds now to ensure a bountiful harvest or successful venture, and then let the ideas you have been seeding take root. Work on manifesting that which you are passionate about. This is what is so special about you and gives you a powerful ability that artificial intelligence doesn't have. Have faith in this.

Nurture and encourage the development of your creative seeds so they will bravely burst forth and sprout, but don't stop there. Great things often require commitment and hard work. Eventually, your projects will have grown strong and can flow freely into the Terrestrial World and flourish. They can then reach up into the Stellar World and affect every other living thing in the field of universal consciousness. Think of that and go for it!

Neo-Mythic Bridge

Brigid feels the murmurations of the starlings vibrate through her being. Every year, tens of thousands of starlings fly in unified rapture to create organic shapes and forms that ebb and flow over the Somerset levels. Imbolc is known as the feast day of St. Brigid. Lambs are being birthed in the field and snowdrops are emerging from the cold soil. Brigid has gathered reeds to make her green crosses, celebrating vibrant new life to come.

23. THE INITIATION OF ARTHUR

...

Conquer Your Fear

THINK ABOUT THE INITIATIONS IN YOUR LIFE AND how they have radically altered your perception. You can never go back to who you were, only forward from who you are now. The obstacles you encounter and overcome are considered initiations. They are not always elaborate rituals designed for such a purpose, and the positive experiences you have also count.

You are moving through an initiatory experience now. There is much wisdom and liberation in not reacting and collapsing into fear during this time, but instead, remaining in a state of conscious awareness. Keeping a cool head and being able to control your emotions is key. This practice will help you develop a mode of thinking and behaving that is deliberately different from your previous modes of thought and behavior. No one can teach this to you and there are no shortcuts. When you come out the other end, this transformation will lead you through the veils to a new, larger life and expression.

Neo-Mythic Bridge

Arthur, as future king, would go through the wild-hunt initiation to encounter the hidden aspects of self and conquer them. The courage to confront his fears was necessary to enter into the Otherworld soulstream of his ancestral power.

24. BELTANE

...

Fertility

New beginnings are at hand. It's a good time to manifest prosperity and fertility in your home environment and beyond. Dormant emotions are ready to grow and flourish in the fecund landscape of your mind and heart. Find time to welcome the changing of the seasons. Honor the awakening new life within you and around you. Alone or with a partner, create an altar of greenery, fairy cakes, and honeymead decorated with symbols dedicated to the Goddess and burgeoning life. Where possible, plant flower and vegetable seeds in your garden that will attract bees, abundance, and love. Build a bonfire or light a candle to signify the transition of the soul seasons in your life and the cleansing of your energy field. Let all your worries and cares rise up with the flame. Welcome the beginning of an internal summer, knowing the ideas and projects that have been sleeping are also ready to come to fruition from the darkness into the light. Celebrate your life and the magical alchemy of Avalon.

Neo-Mythic Bridge

Beltane is the time of lovers and enchantment. The ancient pagan fertility rites start at the Glastonbury Market Cross. The Winter King is bid farewell, then the new May King and Queen are carried up through the town to the White Spring well house across the road from the Red Spring of Chalice Well. Inside the magical stone cavern, they bless the waters to ensure the fertility of the coming seasons. After the pagan ritual, they come out and rejoin the dancing and drumming, the procession making its way into the Bushy Combe meadow where the maypole is raised and the festivities continue.

25. THE NINE MORGANS

...

Light Your Inner Fire

EXPRESS YOUR JOY AND APPRECIATION! FOCUS ON positive manifestations for yourself and others, for the bountiful cornucopia will be enhanced by sharing it with kindred spirits. The group energy around the Lammas fire is very powerful! Now is a good time to express your love and inner fire to another and have it reciprocated. Harvest time is joyful with the satisfaction of an abundant crop. It is when you can turn your mind to your own fulfillment and desires.

Light the eternal flame of Avalon in your heart! Focus on this dynamic fire when you need a boost in vitality. Feel a warm sensation in your chest whenever you tune in to the priestesses and the magical energy of Avalon. Visualize the procession of the nine fire maidens holding their flaming torches high as they approach the waiting pile of the Lammas logs. Call on them now — they are your own nine muses living and breathing in this oracle to send you an inspiring message: Follow your passion, and dance in ecstasy and gratitude for life itself.

Neo-Mythic Bridge

A ninefold sisterhood presides over the Isle of Apples (Avalon). Trained by Morgan le Fay in healing modalities, they also personify inspiration and the creative arts such as music, poetry, and dance — like the nine muses of Greek mythology. It is said the Morgans can also shapeshift and manipulate the weather, and they embody the oracle divination skills of prophecy. For 15,000 years, these priestesses and muses have been remembered in myth, story, and art worldwide, being the oldest known cultural group and seat of learning.

26. LUGHNASA

...

Abundance and Bounty

Celebrate. Things are ripe now. Primal passions are also stirring and coming to fruition. Do not wait too long to gather in the bountiful harvest! If you do, some opportunities will have passed and will not return. Express your positive intentions by creating an abundant altar of seasonal fruit and vegetables. Stand in front of your display, give thanks to the plant devas and nature spirits, and visualize your desires being gratified.

This is also traditionally the time of year when your life is full and you can take time off and relax. Create space for this now, no matter when you pull this card. Focus on your relationships, yourself, or perhaps your family. Go on a vacation if you can; feel and embody the infinite love and abundance in nature. Travel to somewhere new and experience tastes and smells, visions and vistas you have never seen before. Then return home refreshed. Remember to share your bounty with others and just keep what you need.

Neo-Mythic Bridge
Lughnasa honors the sun god Lugh (light) and Grianne, the goddess of grain. It is the time of the first grain harvest of summer. The precious kernels and seeds of wheat, barley, oats, and corn were traditionally harvested at dawn, then baked into bread for the celebration. Children would participate in the festivities, teaching them appreciation for Mother Goddess and the divine life force in all nature.

27. BRIGANTIA

⋯

Wealth

You have been waiting so long to realize your dreams and fulfill your destiny. The goddess Brigantia, queen of the summer lands, brings you gold and honey. Prosperity is very close. Your life will soon change for the better, bringing well-being and happiness to you and those you love. Abundance and wealth can be used in constructive ways to bring your projects and ideas to fruition. Money is a vehicle of energy, usually necessary to acquire materials for building, education to learn a new skill, or just to travel and experience places and sacred sites that will enhance your life and foster creativity.

Some in your current circle of friends may get jealous or resentful of your newfound wealth, but if you treat them with kindness, they will soon see the good and partake in your joy. If not, you may choose not to keep them close. You will attract other like-minded souls into your life through co-creation and shared positive intentions as you spread your wings and soar!

Neo-Mythic Bridge

The goddess Brigantia holds sovereignty over the three worlds. Her sea dragons—the plesiosaurs from the Otherworld—were found near the base of the Tor in the River Brue. Scientists have fondly named the dinosaurs they found there Avalonianus and Camelotia. Her friends from the Stellar World emerge through the portal as she commands respect from the Terrestrial World, seated on her golden throne.

28. THE THREE GRAILS

...

Clear the Mist

DISSOLVE THE MIST TO LOOK AT YOUR SITUATION from every angle. Phenomena can change in character through our thoughts and perceptions. You may think of the Grail as one thing, but it has many aspects: The Druids' 'Cauldron of Plenty'; Mary Magdalene as the vessel of holy blood; and the chalice of the Christians. The Avalon continuum can be accessed by focusing your intent on a particular moment or idea. Be aware of influences from the past and attachments you may have picked up along the way, so you can consider all perspectives equally. Sometimes you must revisit past judgments and reassess why you came to that decision or conclusion in the first place. You are free to change your mind about something as more knowledge surfaces, because you know that ignorance is not bliss. We all keep learning and growing — that's why we are here. When you find out new information about something you formerly believed to be true, assimilate that knowledge to enhance your life experience and allow a new vision to come through.

Neo-Mythic Bridge

The Avalon continuum is a coherent collection of elements and events that shift and change with what we label as 'time'. This spot on the earth has seen so many paradigms acted out upon it. The location of Arthur and Guinevere's grave at Glastonbury Abbey has been proven accurate (as far as it can be by archaeologists).

29. AVNOVA

...

Go with Your Flow

BE LIKE FLOWING WATER MOVING SMOOTHLY OVER obstacles, changing form and adapting to the inconsistent weather in your life; freezing, melting, pooling, then becoming fluid and moving again. Use the resiliency of nature as your guide and ally. Everything in your world may be changing daily, even perceptions you once believed to be true or that you used to depend on. You may find you are constantly readjusting yourself to create some order and understanding out of the chaos of these times.

Take it day by day. Be easy on yourself. Relax and accept a situation rather than trying to alter or control it — unless it will do harm to you or someone else. You may have to wait until things settle down to make plans or pursue a new project. If things do not stabilize soon, and you do move forward, make sure you have alternate backup plans in place. It's helpful to be prepared if you need to pivot direction.

NEO-MYTHIC BRIDGE
The goddess Avnova is known by many names. In the Black Forest of Germany, she is called Abnoba. She is the patroness of waterways, the arteries through which the ancients traded and traveled. They migrated to Britain, where the root word can still be heard even in Avalon. Avnova is thought to be the namesake of the Avon River in England.

30. EPONA

...

Guardianship

REMEMBER TO TAKE CARE OF CREATURES LARGE and small. Be responsible, even if an animal is not your own. Don't be afraid to speak out to protect a defenseless creature or child that cannot speak for itself. No act of kindness goes unnoticed by Source. Let your heart be filled with the strength of the goddess Epona.

You can make a protective charm with her name on it — one for yourself, and one with the image or name of your pet engraved on it. Ask Epona to safeguard your animal friend. Place your sacred amulet either on your altar or where your pet sleeps. Being a guardian is no small thing. Epona is needed again today to protect animals from abuse and extinction.

As the patron of horses and their riders, her protection extends to travelers, ensuring safe passage and guidance for you on any upcoming journeys, near or far. Epona's connection to the Stellar World also suggests her ability to communicate divine messages through your dreams and send prophetic visions to help and protect you on your travels.

Neo-Mythic Bridge

Epona was originally a Celtic goddess, and the only one to be adopted by the Roman Empire. She was the protectress of horses and mules, and the travelers who rode them. Revered and considered an important goddess in her own right, she retained her original form and was not paired up with any Roman deity.

31. THE EGG STONE

...

Make a Wish

The egg stone is a conduit to the Goddess or Divine Feminine. Every wish and prayer you ask of her will be heard if you are sincere. Be as specific as possible in what you are asking for. If you use a sacred space you are familiar with, it will help to focus your attention and intent. Visualize your wish in color and detail, to make it as real as possible. Believe it has already come true, but don't be attached to the way it comes true. It may manifest in circumstances you could not have imagined or would not believe possible.

Knowing this, be aware of everything and everyone around you, so you do not miss the opportunity to receive what you asked for. Of course, the old adage, "Be careful what you wish for, as it may come true," is a good saying to ponder also. Make sure your prayer is for the highest good and does no harm. That said, drawing this card indicates the magic is flowing in your life, so stay positive and see what happens!

Neo-Mythic Bridge

The egg stone in Glastonbury Abbey was found by the psychic archaeologist, Frederick Bligh Bond. It was considered a pre-Roman 'cult stone' or omphalos. This symbolized the ritual center of a sacred enclosed area. The egg-shaped stone was hewn by hand into this form. It has a libation hole in the top for a candle or offerings to the Mother Goddess.

32. BECKERY AND THE BLUE SPRING

• • •

New Insights Are Revealed

TAKE THE TIME NEEDED TO FIGURE THINGS out. Remember, knowledge is power. A new understanding about you, or those around you, will be gained as you put the puzzle pieces together. Your own perception of the past is not carved in stone. Let it be altered as new information comes to light. You may have to give up some idealized notions that no longer serve you but support a false paradigm. It can be difficult to do this as the ego likes to be 'right'. The blue bowl that was found in the Blue Spring was not the Holy Grail, as some would prefer to believe. Finding out the truth about something in your life is better than being misled, as this can create unnecessary, time-consuming detours.

Neo-Mythic Bridge

At the end of Magdalene Street, across from Wearyall Hill, was a chapel dedicated to Mary Magdalene. It was built around one stone-lined grave. The land had been a sacred shrine since Neolithic times. St. Brigid came from Ireland in 488 CE to stay at Beckery (sometimes called 'Bride's Mound'). After her visit, the chapel of Mary Magdalene was rededicated to St. Brigid.

33. SONG OF BRANWEN

...

Sing, Even if Your Heart Is Breaking

LACK OF COMMUNICATION CAN LEAD TO DISCORD. Don't take power or position for granted. Talk to the people involved and use your mediation skills to head off the downward spiral before it gains too much momentum. Misunderstandings can cause havoc in the Terrestrial World, so use the discernment and the wisdom of your higher self when relating with others. Seek guidance if necessary to help avert a crisis.

Bran, brother of Branwen, was a peacemaker and used diplomacy whenever he could, but it was like casting pearls before swine. Eventually, the brother and sister were brought down by the actions of others, including family members. Be careful not to get caught up in the dramas and affairs of those around you. They may try to draw you in as allies, but unless you can actually help and alter the circumstances, it is best to stay clear of the conflict.

Neo-Mythic Bridge

Branwen was considered by many to be the most beautiful maiden in the world. She was the daughter of Llyr, who was the King of all Britons. Her brother was called Bran the Blessed, as his name meant 'blessed raven'. The brother and sister were considered good gods of music and song. They seemed to be giants or titans on the earth, while their half-brothers may have had mixed genetics, causing some of the very human events in their tragic tale.

34. CELTIC SHAMANKA

...

Don Your Spiritual Armor

BE AWARE THAT NOT EVERYONE SUPPORTS YOUR highest expression. Let the harshness of the world and others' criticisms bounce off your protective shield. You can successfully deflect them. Use your psychic inner magic to visualize spheres of light containing your Otherworld allies, coming in to surround and protect you, your home, and your loved ones. They are ready to help when called upon. Like the Shamanka of old, you have the knowledge and power to ward off negative influences. Her secret is having a sense of balance through integrated connections to the three worlds.

Emulate the Celtic Shamanka. She has her feet firmly planted on the surface of Terra while her antlered staff and her higher mind reach into the Stellar World. The use of ritual is recommended to give you a focal point of attention for this work. Create a personal altar with things gathered from nature or from your own unique experiences. This sacred space will build up energy and momentum over time that will enhance your visionary process and telepathic communication, while also manifesting a powerful protective barrier. Remember, focus is key.

Neo-Mythic Bridge

The word Shamanka, like the silver branch of bells, came originally from the Altai Mountains in Siberia. Perhaps the bells were first brought by the reindeer people when they laid out the pathways in the British Isles. These bells were incorporated into the Celtic pantheon and used in ritual from ancient times. Shaking the bells at the four corners alerted the worlds that the Shamanka was ready to traverse between them.

35. GREEN MEN OF GLASTONBURY

...

Share the Load with Joy

A GROUP OF LIKE-MINDED INDIVIDUALS PULLING together can turn a heavy task into a gratifying achievement. It's time to rejoice in the power of community. On May Day, for instance, a joyous group of men, women, and children form a circle around the maypole, weaving the brightly colored ribbons over and under in an ecstatic dance of delight and jubilation.

Participate and feel the essence of Mother Nature burgeoning around you as the darkness of an inner winter recedes. Give yourself the opportunity to meet and commune with others. Reach out and join in. Take part in a community project or celebration. The successful result will be a source of pleasure for all, as your input and strength of purpose will add to the group synergy. You may surprise yourself when you realize that strangers are just friends you haven't met yet. Your soulmate may even be among them!

Neo-Mythic Bridge

The Green Men of Glastonbury celebrate the Divine Masculine. Their knowledge of their part in creation provides a sense of balance. On Beltane, the Green Men dress in elaborate costumes of leaves, green paint, and foliage, delighting the hordes of visitors and locals as they carry the huge maypole through the town. The merrymakers join in with drumming and chanting.

Card Meanings

Stellar World Cards

36. ELEN OF THE WAYS

•••

Lead

BE THE WISE FACILITATOR FOR OTHERS TO FOLLOW. Use discernment in marking out that path, leading others on a positive journey to a worthwhile destination. Let Elen be a role model for you in your chosen practice. Include her knowledge from the Stellar World as well as a practical, grounded vision for the pathways you and your tribe follow. Balance is the key to unity in your group.

Another attribute of a true leader is letting all voices be heard and all needs be considered. This responsibility is not a small one. Yet, the pathways Elen and her people marked out are still visible as highways today. So what you decide to teach your followers could last a very long time and become part of the fabric of the landscape — and the evolution of humanity.

Neo-Mythic Bridge

Elen of the Ways has a history going back to the Paleolithic era. She is the antlered goddess of flight linked to the celestial swan of the star system Cygnus. In recent times, science has detected that the star Cygnus X-3 is emitting cosmic rays directly at Earth that penetrate deep underground. These rays are thought to have been a catalyst for human evolution! On the ground, Elen wore the antlers of a female reindeer. She was the Matron of the trackways that have become roads across Ireland, Britain, and Europe.

37. THE ARRIVAL OF THE TUATHA DÉ DANANN

...

Adapt to a New Location

Moving can be chaotic, but it doesn't have to be. Whether the move is from a job, situation, or dwelling, embrace the change. You have the ability to acclimate to new surroundings where subtle energies will inspire you. Exposure to unfamiliar territory will stimulate and enhance your life in new ways. There are areas of the world where, if you are sensitive, the Tuatha Dé Danann (or off-worlders) will make their presence known to you. It might be a clairaudient experience or a physical manifestation. These occur most clearly at night when forms are best delineated against the darkness. The archetype you receive from the Otherworld could be a thought or idea that has lain dormant for several incarnations, but is to become manifest now through your connection to the Fey and the energy of Avalon. What you do with this new information will have a profound effect on those around you. People will be in awe of the magic imbued in your new creative pursuits, projects, and business ventures.

Neo-Mythic Bridge
The Tuatha Dé Danann arrived in ships coming out of dark clouds in the sky and landed on the mountaintops of Ireland. Some stayed there while others went on to Britain and Egypt. They were a tall, beautiful race with an ethereal glow. With their technologies, it is not hard to imagine their involvement in building unexplained stone cairns and monuments. This race traversed the three worlds, coming from the Stellar World, landing on Terra, then retreating into the inner earth, where

tunnels connected them to other lands. A network of tunnels exists under Glastonbury Tor in Avalon, where sightings and various phenomena have been reported through the ages.

38. CAER ARIANRHOD

...

Inspiration and Initiation

Dare to do what inspires you. If it doesn't work out, you will learn from it. If it does work out, you will be enriched in many ways, so you have nothing to lose. Do something you have always wanted to do. If you are clearly motivated, explore your skills and talents. As long as it does no harm to others, ignore any potential opposition from friends and family. Test yourself and push yourself forward like the poets, artists, and magicians of old, who dared to visit the land of Caer Arianrhod and her spinning fortress. Inspiration and initiation can be acquired from stepping into the unknown and following your dreams. There is the danger of not returning, but when a decision is made and a step is taken, you can never go back to the way things were before, anyway. If you cave into fear, you will never know what might have transpired, and you will always wonder. As in the hero's journey, the stories and knowledge you bring back from your travels will teach and inspire others.

Neo-Mythic Bridge

The Celtic star goddess, Arianrhod, is said to inhabit a spinning fortress bridging the three worlds. It exists in all three realms at the same time. It is said to be connected to Atlantis. Caer Arianrhod was considered the land of death, rebirth, and inspiration. If they dared, artists, poets, and magicians went there for training and initiations. Those who survived returned to tell their stories and to teach and inspire others, for they were now endowed with clear sight, the gift of prophecy, and silver tongues!

39. MORGAN, HIGH PRIESTESS OF AVALON

...

Secret Sanctum

KEEP THE DIVINE FEMININE/MASCULINE MYSTIQUE about you. Not everything has to be revealed; it is good to keep a little mystery about your life. To protect the sacredness of your seedling ideas, plans, or relationships, step away from the mundane world around you and go into your own private, inner space. It is best to keep your own counsel at this time, sequestered in your sanctum. Doing this will support the energies trying to help and advise you to stay close by but hidden from view. It will also be a barrier to the possibly critical or discouraging opinions of others at this delicate stage of the creation process. This encouragement of solitude is wisdom from the High Priestess, and is necessary to follow at the moment. When the time is right, you will know when to open up your sphere to the world again, trusting that what you have grown is strong enough to weather any storms.

Neo-Mythic Bridge

It is said Morgan was a High Priestess of Atlantis who brought her tools, abilities, and knowledge to the Isle of Avalon. The receding tides of water, combined with the ethereal mists, made the Tor hill appear and disappear like it was floating in and out of the Otherworld. This shifting landscape made locating Morgan's realm of Avalon difficult and provided protection for Morgan and her priestesses, keeping the uninitiated at bay.

40. ARCHANGEL MICHAEL

...

Justice

ARCHANGEL MICHAEL APPEARS TO YOU ABOVE Glastonbury Tor, wielding his flaming sword of truth. He bears the message that justice will be done and balance will be restored to your life, but you must take action yourself. Pick up that shining sword and cut away all the excess baggage, negative influences, and whatever is not needed or necessary to create the positive existence you deserve. Anybody who has wronged you or attempted to undermine your power cannot harm you now, so grasp your flaming sword, hold it high, and clean house energetically. It's time to live in a higher state of vibration where draconian and lower energy forms cannot operate. Michael is a very high-dimensional being, and he has your back. Remember that and proceed without fear.

Neo-Mythic Bridge

In early times, mountains, hills, and high places were dedicated to Archangel Michael. He is a warrior for protection and truth. Archangel Michael transcends religions and is present in many belief systems. The ley line dedicated to him runs through Britain. It was marked out by stone circles and monuments, including Glastonbury Tor and St. Michael's Mount in Cornwall. The alignment may have been established during the Neolithic period. Later, churches were built over them to use or transmute the energy.

41. TAYGETAN WARRIOR

...

Assistance Is at Hand

Ask for help, then pay attention. You do not know in what form it will come — you may benefit from adapting to things outside your comfort zone. Expand your awareness to include the Stellar World. Listen carefully to the answers and directions from your star family, for they are all around you. You may be given an assignment to participate in the changes that are taking place.

You are an immortal spirit dwelling temporarily in a third-dimensional body. You have a unique frequency and soul signature that is yours alone. Your DNA is like a biological internet. There are symbols and codes spliced into it for recognition and communication with the Stellar World. This coding identifies your galactic origins and is carried within you through lifetimes. Your star family can read this code, and they are waiting for you to awaken and remember, so you are able to interact with them and receive their assistance.

Neo-Mythic Bridge

Unidentified Anomalous Phenomena (UAP, previously UFO) sightings over Glastonbury Tor are commonplace and have been observed as far back as records were written and events were painted. As in the saying, "As above, so below," there are conflicts throughout the densities of the stellar realms. There is a war going on above, as is below, one affecting the other. Fortunately, there are humanoid beings who are related to us and consider us family. They are endeavoring to assist.

42. ANGEL OF CHALICE WELL

...

Speak Your Truth

Do not hold back what needs to be said. It is not healthy for you to keep things inside. Expressing what you believe to be true could alter the decisions of others and change their lives as well as your own. The lion's head at Chalice Well represents the throat chakra of the body. It is a place of remembrance and speech. Focus on that image before you speak.

Contemplate the perspective of the angel and the lion from each one's vantage point, remembering that the mixing of the red and white waters of Avalon creates balance.

Where possible, make sure there is crystal clarity in the words you choose. Try not to slander or hurt anyone, as that always has repercussions. Talking about it will be a great relief to you. Unload your burden on a trusted friend who will really listen and not judge. After your discussion, you may arrive at a different way of viewing the situation, or talking may even defuse it. Take a deep breath and express yourself!

Neo-Mythic Bridge

The flow of the waters in Glastonbury's Chalice Well Gardens are arranged like the chakras of the body. The angel sitting above the lion's head pours water from the White Spring out of her grail into the Red Spring as an alchemical marriage of polarities. The union of the red and white waters creates enhanced healing properties for opening the gate of remembrance and expression without fear.

43. SILBURY STARGATE

...

Think Outside the Flock

DON'T BE AFRAID OF RIDICULE IF YOU RELATE your own experiences. They will be like seeds, opening the minds of others to new thoughts and possibilities. Help others step over the threshold into the reality that we are not alone in the universe. The Druids and Celts include the Stellar Realms in their teachings, as do the Hopi, Dogon, Huichol, Egyptians, and Indigenous Australians, just to name a few. Study star knowledge. It is written, painted, and carved into many areas of Mother Gaia. Seeing and internalizing the symbols will act as a catalyst for you, expanding your consciousness and the way you view your own world (and its relationship to the Stellar World). The art left behind still contains the vibration of its creator; the images live in your Sourcefield to be accessed at any time to inspire you and teach the wisdom of the three worlds. This new understanding will open up the possibility of contact with the star people, if you wish it.

Neo-Mythic Bridge

Several policemen in the Avebury area of Wiltshire, England, have reported unexplained incidents and encounters with non-terrestrial life forms. One group of off-worlders they observed emerged from a portal or stargate across from Silbury Hill. The description fits the "tall whites": alien humanoids who are 6 to 10 feet tall with very thin bodies, transparent blond hair, and very large blue eyes.

44. CHALICE WELL CONTINUUM

...

You Are the Oracle

THE GREAT GODDESS SITS IN SILENT REVERENCE IN the Chalice Well, remembering the past and future. She calls you to study with her so that in time, you will master this method of communication as her adept and become your own oracle. Visualize and embody the Goddess of Avalon now, then ask your questions. Listen to the guidance given.

The Goddess is directly linked to our deepest spiritual origins. She knows all because she traverses the three worlds. The Stellar World, the Terrestrial World, and the Otherworld are all interconnected in harmony in the veins of Gaia. You, animals, plants, and other sensitive creatures can tune in to the frequencies of these currents and communicate through them. It is very much like a galactic internet.

Drink sacred water and attune yourself to the harmonic frequencies flowing through our planet. Wisdom and answers will come. All is there for you.

Neo-Mythic Bridge
Before the beginning of history, there was a red spring now called Chalice Well. The Druids established a college there, recognizing the telluric energies of what is now called the Michael and Mary lines as conducive to their teachings. The two dance around each other in the garden, creating a healing magnetism.

ABOUT THE AUTHOR/ARTIST

• • •

CHERYL YAMBRACH ROSE is a portrait painter, visionary artist, and the author of the book *Art Through the Eyes of the Soul* (foreword by Dr. Jean Houston). She paints in oils on linen in a synthesis of the old-master style and her own unique technique of tuning in through the eyes. Excelling in spiritual portraiture, Cheryl is collected by many discerning luminaries, including Gary Zukav and Neale Donald Walsch. Her artwork has been published and shown worldwide, including in the Nelson Rockefeller Collection, the Rosicrucian Egyptian Museum, and the San Francisco Palace of Fine Arts. It has been featured on the Wisdom and Travel Channels, and is included in a book of the top 100 living Western artists. In England, Cheryl has been published by Thames and Hudson, Blandford, Watkins, and others. Cheryl is featured in the Chinese film *Awakening Journey*, which also features Neale Donald Walsch and Dr. Bruce Lipton.

Cheryl has created numerous oracle decks, including *Through the Eyes of the Soul*, *Art Through the Starstream*, *Transcendent Journeys*, and *The*

Mystique of Magdalene. Her work has been translated into French, Chinese, Japanese, Czech, and German, and in 2016, she won a 'Visionary Product of the Year' award at INATS in Denver.

Her spiritual portraits are multi-dimensional paintings, incorporating information accessed through the sight of the pineal gland or inner eye as it connects to the Sourcefield. Founder of Neo-Mythic Art®, she brings forth images out of the morphic fields surrounding sacred sites and the vortices within them.

"The purpose of visionary art and artists is to make ourselves as receptive a vehicle as possible to bring back high ideals and images to manifest on the physical plane. The artist must be able to traverse between the worlds, yet become resident to none. As an artist, my highest aspiration is the infusion of Spirit into matter."

Cheryl lives and works in Glastonbury, England, and Mt. Shasta, California. Visit her online at:

www.cherylrose.com

Also available from Blue Angel®

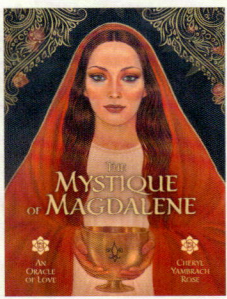

THE MYSTIQUE OF MAGDALENE
An Oracle of Love
Cheryl Yambrach Rose

Beloved teacher, practical mystic, and divine healer Mary Magdalene is an archetype for our time. Within her journeys, we discover the stories, secrets, and potentials of all women who rise above challenges using intuition, creative thinking, and deep, transformative compassion. Through the text and vision of Cheryl Yambrach Rose, we can enter the warmth of safety of Magdalene's sacred aura, share in her travels, and be blessed by her sweet revelation.

44 Cards & Guidebook Set • ISBN: 978-1-922573-31-5

Also available from Blue Angel®

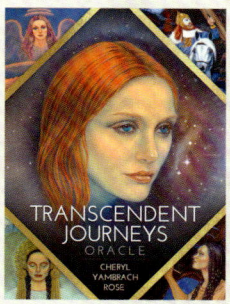

TRANSCENDENT JOURNEYS ORACLE
Cheryl Yambrach Rose

Cheryl Yambrach Rose's images are described as direct portals to the profound and enlightening moments, mentors, messengers, and magic the world needs right now. Work with this deck to bridge worlds, deepen connections, and awaken your soul to a higher vibration. This 45-card deck is lovingly attuned with the Pleiades, ancient teachings and present-day revelation to bring you clarity, direction, and inspiration for the good of all. The guidebook includes simple instructions on how to use this oracle with layouts and meanings to activate your intuitive processes.

45 Cards & Guidebook Set • ISBN: 978-1-925538-81-6

Also available from Blue Angel®

THROUGH THE EYES OF THE SOUL
52 Prophecy Cards & Guidebook
Cheryl Yambrach Rose

Reach into myth, knowing, and wonder with this luminescent oracle from celebrated visionary Cheryl Yambrach Rose. This set provides an energetic link to divine beings, sacred sites, and otherworldly spaces so you can access meaningful answers and direction.

Set includes 52 prophecy cards and an illustrated guidebook for actualizing wisdom & weaving your destiny every day.

52 Cards & Guidebook Set • ISBN: 978-0-6487467-9-9

Also available from Blue Angel®

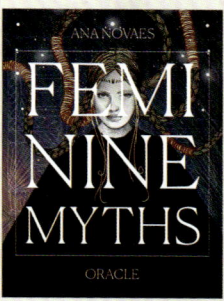

FEMININE MYTHS ORACLE
Ana Novaes

In this boldly illustrated oracle, feminine deities across many cultures have been uniquely reimagined with a surrealist twist to inspire your multi-faceted gifts.

Traditional maidens, mothers and crones as well as enigmatic heroines and gender-fluid spirits dance through this deck. Celebrate the many faces, bodies and colors of the feminine, while witnessing your own dynamic beauty and divine potential in their reflection.

50 Cards & Guidebook Set • ISBN: 978-1-922574-29-9

Notes

Notes

For more information on this
or any Blue Angel Publishing® release,
please visit our website at:

www.blueangelonline.com